CW01645164

Colophon

Published by Colophon Print
www.colophonprint.com

Renting HMOs SUSSED
A practical guide to managing an HMO
(House of Multiple Occupation)

Copyright © 2012 HMO Landlady and Ben Reeve-Lewis

ISBN: 978-0-9561210-5-9

All rights reserved. No part of this publication may be reproduced, stored in a retrieval system, or transmitted in any form or by any means, electronic, mechanical, photocopy, recording, or otherwise, without the prior written permission of the copyright owner.

A CIP catalogue record for this book is available from the British Library.

Renting HMOs -Sussed

A practical guide to managing an HMO

(House of Multiple Occupation)

HMO Landlady
with Ben Reeve-Lewis

SUSSED
100 Pages of Personal Experience

Limit of Liability

Though both publisher and author have applied their best efforts to prepare this book, neither make any representations or warranties with respect to the accuracy or completeness of its contents, specifically disclaiming any implied warranties of performance or fitness for a particular purpose. The accuracy and completeness of the contents and the opinions stated are not guaranteed or warranted to produce any particular results, nor may the advice and strategies provided be suitable for every individual. Neither publisher nor author shall be liable for any loss of profit or any other commercial damages, including but not limited to special, incidental, consequential, or other damages

Introduction

Welcome to Renting HMOs SUSSED

Welcome to Renting HMOs Sussed which has been written to walk you through setting up and effectively managing your House of Multiple Occupation with advice on how to stay on the right side of the law whilst keeping your tenants happy and safe.

Fresh off the Internet search engines after typing in "HMO", I've discovered that there are dozens of websites offering "property riches, high yield, low risk, Your Guide to Making £billions through HMOs, etc, etc". There are lots of experienced, excellent HMO landlords and there are also lots of greedy, neglectful ones. If you're considering investing in HMOs, be aware that the job requires responsibility, a sense of humour and a dose of compassion!

There is a whole library of books on the market about HOW to rent a property and these are useful reading for new landlords. However, there's little information giving you practical hints and tips on how to purchase and manage an HMO (House of Multiple Occupation). Yes, they are governed by the same laws and principles as other letting properties, but the reality of being the proud owner of one is very, very different.

This Sussed book is for anyone considering investing in, or who already owns Houses of Multiple Occupation – whether they need to be licenced or not. It draws on five years' worth of experience as an HMO Landlady with the added benefit of advice on how not to fall foul of the law from Ben Reeve-Lewis (tenant/landlord dispute negotiator, housing law trainer and consultant, property journalist and broadcaster).

It highlights the rewards and challenges of owning HMOs, along with tips on how to ride the waves of good and bad tenants.

HMO Landlady

HMO tenants – high maintenance responsibility and source of income

UPERFLY
errea

Contents

Page

Page

Starting Out – HMO Landlady

After deciding on HMOs, the first question that kept me awake at night was "But how do I go about managing the house effectively?". There was no practical advice available on the Internet and I really wanted to ask someone–anyone with experience - particularly about abiding by the law. However, evicting someone from a self-contained property such as a family house or flat is very different from evicting someone who shares a front door and communal space with the very people they are annoying. Flailing around and renting rooms to the first person who came a-knocking with disastrous consequences was stressful, so I've written this Sussed book to give you basic tips and assure you that the problems you may face aren't unique and, with a few pointers, so you will find a way to manage them.

For the latest tenant stories, please visit my blog at ***www.hmolandlady.wordpress.com***

HMO Landlady

WHAT IS AN HMO?

"HMO" is an abbreviation for House of Multiple Occupation. This means that the house is shared by people who represent more than one household, i.e. anyone who has a different surname and is not in a relationship, and has access to all shared areas such as kitchen, bathrooms, hallways and landings.

HMOs only need to be licensed if they are 3 or more storeys tall with 5 or more tenants sharing* - but do check with your local council's Environmental Health Department if your property needs to be licensed. They'll tell you what hoops to jump through, although most councils have made their guidelines available online. If it sounds daunting, don't worry. It may require a bit more investment and some serious schmoozing with council officers, but at least you'll be legal and above board. You will also need to check if your local Council has Article 4 Direction in place BEFORE you buy your property (type "Article 4 Direction" into an Internet search engine to check participating councils). This is a planning law designed to prevent an oversupply of HMOs by requiring a planning application to be submitted to change a property from a dwelling house into an HMO.

**HMO Licensing: like any licence, the council want to check the building is safe to inhabit and ensure the landlord is a "fit and proper person" to be running it, i.e. with no criminal convictions. Different Local Authorities have their own charging structure and guidelines.*

WHY BUY AN HMO AND WHAT DOES IT INVOLVE?

HMOs are typically high yielding investments, unless, of course you have an inside track on the stock market, which will make you far more money in a lot less time without having to be on call 24/7!

If property's your thing though, and you want a guaranteed market demand, enjoy working with people from all walks of life and want a very respectable return to boot, choose HMOs. The figures will of course depend on how much mortgage you take out (if at all), so I've based the example here on a typical house in our area. To get an idea of likely rental charges in *your* area, look in the local paper, or online at:

Gumtree ***(www.gumtree.com)***
or Spare Room ***(www.spareroom.co.uk)***.

WHO IS THE HMO MARKET?

Whatever your personal property investment strategy, it is essential that you KNOW YOUR MARKET. Ask yourself "Who is likely to want to rent a room in my property?" The answer will depend variously on a mix of location, amenities and transport links. Typically your tenants are likely to be:

Students
Transient and foreign workers
People on low wages
LHA (Local Housing Allowance) claimants

But whoever wants a room, remember, it will be all they can afford! When I started out, I had no idea who would want to rent a room in a shared house with complete strangers. My first property came fully tenanted with a Spanish waiter, 2 South African nurses and a Polish couple. At one point I had around 50% LHA claimants, 10% foreign workers and the rest British workers, but only now have 30% LHA claimants due to more working people being able to afford only a room rather than a flat. There are people who will probably be in the house for the rest of their lives, others whose objective is to save hard but mostly tenants will be people who want to pay an all-inclusive rent so they can spend the rest of their disposable income on girlfriends and beer.

PRICES TO CHARGE AND EXPECTED YIELD

Individuals

Here are some example calculations based on a 3 bedroom terraced house bought for £180,000 with a 25% deposit and paid on an interest only basis at 5%.

Note: all rents are inclusive of bills

First floor:

Room 1 (master bedroom – 20 ft x 15 ft):	£100 pw
Room 2 (middle bedroom – 15 ft x 12 ft):	£85 pw
Room 3 (back bedroom – 10 ft x 8 ft):	£70 pw
Room 4 (living room – 17 ft x 15 ft):	£90 pw
Room 5 (dining room – 15 ft x 12 ft):	£85 pw
Total income:	**£430 pw**

Outgoings (Individuals)

Per month	**Per Year**
Mortgage: £625	£7,500
Water and Sewage £50	£600
Internet and telephone £25	£300
Electricity £100	£1,200
Gas £100	£1,200
Council Tax £130 (monthly payments for 10 months)	£1,300
Buildings insurance £25 (monthly payments for 10 months)	£250
Total outgoings £1,055	**£12,350**

Yearly income (£430 x 52 weeks)	£22,360
Yearly outgoings	£12,350
Yield without mortgage and utilities	12.4%
Yield without mortgage	12%
Yield with mortgage and utilities	3.7%

Students

First floor:

Room 1 (master bedroom – 20 ft x 15 ft):	£80 pw
Room 2 (middle bedroom – 15 ft x 12 ft):	£75 pw
Room 3 (back bedroom – 10 ft x 8 ft):	£65 pw
Ground floor:	
Room 4 (dining room – 15 ft x 12 ft):	£75 pw
Room 5 (communal living room/bed – 17 ft x 15 ft):	£75 pw
Total income	**£295 pw**

Outgoings (Individuals)

Per month	**Per Year**
Mortgage: £625	£7,500
Water and Sewage £50	£600
Internet and telephone £25	£300
Buildings insurance £25 (monthly payments for 10 months)	£250
Total outgoings £725	**£8,650**
Yearly income (£295 x 52 weeks)	**£15,340**
(this will depend on the length of contract e.g. academic year only or 12 months)	
Yearly outgoings	£8,650
Yield without mortgage and utilities	8.5%
Yield without mortgage	7.8%
Yield with bills	3.7%

Hard work, but a pretty good return in the current climate and an excellent return if you're smart enough not to have a mortgage! It's also worth noting that the utility costs are fairly similar whether you're running a 4–, 5– or 6– bed HMO.

Maintenance

These figures don't include any maintenance allowances. Unlike letting out residential property to single households, expect to receive higher tenant turnover due to their transient nature of only wanting a room, above average call outs to deal with problems and a higher than average maintenance bill! Oh, and it's wise to make friends with a good locksmith and key cutter as HMO tenants are notorious for losing their keys or forgetting to leave them when abandoning the property.

I don't carry out any maintenance personally so my yearly expenditure of £15,000 is high. If you possess DIY skills and enjoy routing around in cellars, attics and on roofs then you can set your budget lower. Remember though that electrical and gas safety certificates must be carried out by a professional – no matter how competent you are.

PROS AND CONS OF HMO OWNERSHIP

PROS Ability to develop a good relationship: as in any business "people buy people". Tenants are less likely to mess around if they get on well with you.

Maintain control: if you have access to communal areas at any point and collect the rent from a tenant's room, you can judge how well they are looking after the place.

Less risk: if one tenant defaults on his/her payment or a room lies vacant for a while, there's still enough money to pay the mortgage and utilities.

CONS Higher than average maintenance bills – water leaks are the worst.

Hands-on role for the landlord – that's why most estate agents won't touch them as they'd want a lot more than a 10% management fee.

Potential conflict: even though you've reference checked and listened to your gut instinct, if the tenant clashes with other people in the house you have to do everything within your power to restore harmony. In the heat of an argument, I have been known to send tenants to their rooms for time out.

SET UP

Furniture

Both the student market and individuals will expect basic furniture to be provided. Flat packed furniture rarely lasts, breaks when moved around a room and you'll be forever smashing it up and taking it to the tip. Quality wooden second hand furniture is sturdy and survives being moved around to suit the tenant without falling apart. Make friends with your local furniture charity shop such as EMMAUS (www.emmaus.org.uk) or keep an eye out in the classifieds of the local paper.

Rooms should include:

- Bed – preferably wood or metal headboard so it's easy to clean, not upholstered!
- Bedside table
- Lamp
- Wardrobe
- Chest of drawers
- CLEAN carpet
- Curtains are best so they can be washed between tenancies
- Desk and chair – if targeting the student market
- Mattress protector – far cheaper to replace than a mattress

Temperature (Individuals only)

Maintaining an ambient temperature can be tricky if you've got foreign tenants from the northern hemisphere who are positively sweating at 16°C and those from the Southern hemisphere reaching for their thermals if the outside temperature drops below 25°C.

The best advice is to make sure that all doors and windows are properly draught proofed, the temperature can reach and maintain a recommended 20°C and the heating is on when you would expect it to be warm e.g. 6-9 am then 4 pm-10 pm. It's a good idea to discuss with your tenants what suits them best (within reason).

Boilers

Boilers need to be maintained and an annual Gas Safety Certificate must be available for the tenants to view. If you let to students, you'll probably leave the bill to them to sort out between themselves, but when letting to individuals it's easier for you to take charge of the account and factor it into the room rates. Some landlords do expect the individual tenants to pay for the gas via a prepaid keycard but this seems unfair if someone has put £10 on it, only for the other 4 rooms to make use of the hot water and heating for as long as it lasts!!

If you decide to pay the gas bill, the recommendation is to lock the boiler in a cupboard. This prevents tenants fiddling with the controls, potentially breaking it and putting the timer onto constant. A broken boiler is not only dangerous but very expensive to fix.

Thermostats

Again, if the tenants are paying the bill they can have free rein of the thermostat! However, if you're paying, fit a tamper proof thermostat control which allows the tenants to set the temperature between 2 variables e.g. 15° to 23°. This gives them some control but doesn't allow the boiler to attempt to reach 30 degrees every day! Also consider the siting of the thermostat – keep it in the communal area, away from outside walls and, if putting in a hallway, bear in mind that if tenants smoke they tend to do so with the back door wide open thereby lowering the temperature.

Energy Meters

Students: You may decide to provide an energy meter with the house to educate the tenants as to how much it costs to run appliances and help them keep an eye on their spend.

Individuals: It's possible to provide a room with its own meter and the individual room usage is billed directly to the tenant. Spark Energy ***(www.sparkenergy.co.uk)*** is one such company that offers this service.

Internet Access/Telephone Line

These days, everyone expects Wi-Fi Internet access. To avoid disputes, the landlord should pay for the phone line, router and Internet connection, then lock it all away to prevent abuse. There are some great deals in terms of unlimited access, or you can provide the line and let the tenants organise the Internet and split it between themselves.

Décor

Paint all walls in a uniform colour with the same brand of paint! You'd be amazed at how many variations of brilliant white and magnolia there are out there, so find the paint you like and stick to it. This means you can touch up marks, etc., without having to repaint an entire room. Gloss on the woodwork is more durable than eggshell or satin and can be wiped clean. Choose your flooring wisely: laminate/wipe clean in the kitchens and communal areas, hard wearing carpet on the stairs and landing and cheap in the bedrooms. Think "Will it show a stain if a cup of coffee were to be spilt on it?"

Fire Regulations

A non-licenced HMO requires, at the very least, hardwired smoke detectors in the hallway and landing as well as self-closing fire doors to the bedrooms and kitchens. I shy away from fire extinguishers in case they are messed around with, but do provide fire blankets for when a tenant has the midnight munchies, then goes back to sleep having forgotten to turn off his sausages.

Licenced HMOs will require a full fire detection system, call points and emergency lighting. These need to be tested on a regular basis by a competent person or, if you're like me, take the guesswork out of it and buy a maintenance contract from the supplier.

White Goods

Obviously it's only fair that tenants need to cook and wash their clothes. I provide cooker (good quality and cleaned professionally once a year), microwave, toaster, kettle, fridge/freezer and washing machine, but don't supply dishwasher or tumble dryer.

Cleaning

In the early days I used to jump up and down in the hallway bemoaning the state of the bathrooms. FACT: tenants (especially male) don't enjoy cleaning other people's mess and I don't blame them. Provide cleaning equipment and products and, as a back up, hire a cleaner once a week to cover the communal areas.

HOW TO ADVERTISE

Depending on which market you've chosen will determine how you advertise:

Students
Most universities and colleges will have their own accommodation guidelines and deparment. Some landlords have their own websites dedicated to student lettings, availability register and rents. All the details are on the website and they even have their own signage boards.

Individuals
When a room becomes vacant I text all my existing tenants to see if they have a friend looking for a room. A good recommendation is valuable as nice, honest, clean living people tend to attract the same sort. Otherwise, consider advertising in the local paper or subscribing to ***www.spareroom.com.*** Below is some suggested wording:

> **A large, clean room available to rent in quiet, town centre shared house close to railway station and buses.**
> **Rent £xx pw incl all bills, deposit £xxx**
> **Refs required**
> **[Optional] Sorry no DSS**
> **To view contact :**
> **[your telephone number and/or email]**

When a potential tenant calls, have a list of interview questions ready to ask over the phone to check they can provide basic information and, if you're happy with the way the conversation is progressing, agree to meet them. Book appointments, take their details and ask them to contact you if they're going to be late or have found a room elsewhere and have any further questions ready. You'd be amazed how many times I've found myself waiting around for a no show.

LHA/DSS Claimants

Don't discount LHA (Local Housing Allowance) or DSS (Department of Social Security) tenants tenants due to bad press. I've had some great ones and if they are under the age of 35, the current legislation states they are only entitled to a room in a shared house allowance. After all, what would you do if you didn't have a job or a family to fall back on? For some, a room is a palace compared to being homeless.

If you're happy to consider tenants in receipt of housing benefit, it's worth knowing how the system works. Housing allowance is paid 2 or 4 weeks normally in arrears (depending on your council) and the tenant can elect for it to be paid direct to them to pass on, or to ask for it to be paid to you as landlord. Some landlords ask for a deposit and first month's rent which allows the tenant to get the application in and processed hopefully in time for the next rent!

The LHA rate is set across the Council region and can fluctuate, so for up to date information look at your local Council's websites. Depending on how much the tenant is awarded it may be necessary to ask for a top up which they will have to pay you direct out of any other benefits they receive.

STARTING A TENANCY

Choosing A Tenant

Now you're up and running it's time to fill the house. When interviewing prospective tenants and they've passed your verbal interrogation (think Spanish Inquisition), meet them in person and see how they hold up under face to face scrutiny. You need to know you can work and communicate effectively with your tenant. Check they answer your telephone questions again (fibbers will forget what they said the first time), spend time listening to what they have to say, and remember it's OK to ask enough personal questions to gauge their lifestyle. Once you've got a contender, ask them to complete a Tenant Information Form (there's one at the back of this book) for reference check, next of kin info (very, very important if you happen to find their body) and signature for permission to check details. Also look up ***www.landlordreferencing.co.uk*** - a free online check of any rent arrears and damage from the previous landlord.

If they all check out and no one has said "I wondered where they'd turn up, the little *****" and you're happy, offer the room. However, if there is even the SLIGHTEST gut instinct that this person is not all he or she seems – even if you can't put your finger on it – reject them professionally and with courtesy. (I have a list of white lies designed not to offend!). Also bear in mind that their current landlord may be economical with the truth if they're delighted to get rid of the tenant.

Individuals

How you decide a tenant is good for your house will be down to your own criteria. E.g. if you've decided on the DSS market, be prepared for sketchy previous credit history. Foreign workers fresh from abroad probably won't be able to provide previous landlord details and working people may only have just started their job.
Be aware of trying to mix and match too many cultures and types of people in the same house – a labourer showering at 5 am is going to annoy someone in the room next to the bathroom if they've just got to sleep after an evening/night shift as a waiter or carer. Someone who enjoys entertaining the opposite sex late into the night, will come to blows with another tenant who has to get up for work at 6 am, etc. etc. Use your common sense – who would you be happy to share the communal areas with?

Students

Hopefully the group wanting to rent the house will turn up en masse. Their lifestyle and personalities will be less important as they'll already be friends and able to sort out any squabbles between themselves.

Tenancy Agreements

If you're a member of a landlord association you can download tenancy agreements from their websites and some offer Room Agreements. (See chapter below for more details and web addresses). Whichever you decide, the law remains:

1. All agreements are Assured Shorthold Tenancies

2. The landlord must give them a minimum of 6 months fixed term although a tenant can request a shorter term

3. The tenant can give you 1 month's notice at the end of the fixed term, but you must give them no less than 2 months or 8 weeks notice and serve a Section 21 notice if you want to end the tenancy

That's the law and you can't get away with it. However, I appreciate that individual tenants may move in and within the first few weeks not get on with their housemates or get lucky enough to be offered another job elsewhere. I'm realistic that it's futile to hold them to a 6 month fixed term so will accept 2 weeks' notice to vacate. However, this doesn't work the other way round and, if I want them to leave, will abide by the Section 21 law. (more about this later).

Students may fall out with each other – and if one decides to move on, the rest of the house are still liable for the monthly rent regardless if there's an empty room. I strongly suggest that you obtain a guarantor for student lets where the parents/guardians are liable for rent payments and damage costs.

Taking A Deposit

If you take a deposit it MUST be registered within 30 days of receipt with one of the following schemes. If you don't, you can't serve a Section 21 notice and it is, after all, the tenant's bond against damage, not additional rental income!

Here are a few Government approved schemes where the deposit can be lodged.

Some schemes are insurance based which means that you pay to register the deposit but keep it until returned to the tenant:

1) The Dispute Service
   www.thedisputeservice.co.uk

2) My Deposits
   www.mydeposits.co.uk

However, the Deposit Protection Service ***www.depositprotection.com*** is a custodial scheme which is free to use and the landlord gives the money to the DPS to safeguard until the end of the tenancy.

Follow the instructions on the websites which will give you all the information to provide the tenant as to where their deposit is held. Remember – the Prescribed Information MUST be given along with the deposit certificate which is available to download after you've registered.

Inventories

In order to claim monies against a deposit you need to provide proof that damage has occurred. Take a photo or video footage of the room, ask the tenant to sign a condition form which should also list any furniture in the room. According to the deposit companies, décor has a life expectancy e.g. 4 years for bedroom walls, etc. so be realistic when claiming against a deposit. It's not fair to deduct normal wear and tear if a tenant has been there more than a year – you'd have had to paint the room to freshen it up for another tenant anyway.

RULES OF THE HOUSE

By now, as with any household, it's wise to establish a set of Rules. Here's an example of mine:

1. Please have your rent ready by 9.30 am every Saturday unless you have made an alternative agreement with me (e.g. paying monthly). If you cannot pay you must call or text me BEFORE Saturday with a good reason and date when you can pay.

2. No smoking anywhere in the house – it's the law!

3. Clean up after yourself in the bathroom AND the kitchen.

4. If I call or text you and you don't answer, I would appreciate you contacting me within 24 hours via text, phone, email or carrier pigeon if necessary.

5. I will collect your rent from a pre-agreed location (bed, bedside table, etc.) Please don't ask me hunt for it in dirty sheets or your pants drawer – I am NOT your mother!

6. If you decide to ignore me or fail to pay your rent, I will not beat you with a base ball bat or send in the heavy mob, but I WILL nag you, sit outside your room until you appear, call your next of kin and report you missing and follow all the legal eviction channels (Section 8 and Section 21 Notices - Housing Act 1987).

7. Please put some clothes on before you answer your door to me.

EFFECTIVE MANAGEMENT OF AN HMO

Rent Collecting and Service Calls

The reason most people shy away from this market is that they fear the complexities and time consuming management. If letting the house on a single assured shorthold tenancy to say, students, collecting the rent will be monthly and you won't need to visit the property except when things go wrong. If, on the other hand, you are renting to individuals you will probably find yourself at the property several times a month.

Individuals

The majority of my rents are due on a weekly basis one week in advance. Most people get paid on a Friday so I make sure that I am there at 9.30 am on a Saturday morning before they've had a chance to spend it in the pub. Some get paid monthly or four weekly, so I collect the day after they are paid and the tenants receiving LHA payments receive their money from the council 2 weeks in arrears. You need a receipt book and diary to note when each rent is due and how much, which minimises any discrepancy.

Students

Payment by standing order from either the parents' account or students' minimises your having to chase rent. If you've ever been a student in higher education staying away from home – draw on your own experiences! Some people prefer to let to girls only, in the belief that they are tidier and cleaner than boys, who think nothing of wading their way through empty beer cans in the hallway and leaving their dirty laundry out for mum to deal with at the end of each term. I leave this one to your own judgement.

Pets

Pets are NOT suitable for shared accommodation. Don't get me wrong, I live with a dog, cat and 2 guinea pigs and love animals but not everyone does. It's unfair to allow a tenant to move in with a cat if someone else in the house is allergic to fur, or for a tenant to keep a cuddly boa constrictor only to find it escaping and popping up in the toilet pan. One of my tenants feeds a tame seagull from his bedsit roof which is great until he's woken by the relentless tapping on the window at 5 am!

What Do You Do if a Tenant Has a Child?

Now, tenants with children come in different formats: girl gets pregnant whilst in a house share, families can only afford one room (I often find this of foreign sounding applicants so maybe they don't qualify for housing benefit help?) or, typically, bloke has been ejected from his marriage and home for a variety of reasons and desperately wants access to his child. We have a house which I renamed "Fathers For Justice" House as all the tenants were 20-30 years old, had fallen foul of the missus, lost all their money as I'm guessing their other half dealt with the finances and all they had left was a suitcase, a battered ego and a promise of child access.

Stories

Jason: turned up on the doorstep clutching my phone number exactly 3 years ago this month. He had no money, a pile of debt, an angry ex-wife and two children. He'd been recommended by an existing tenant and, as regular readers of my blog know, I'm a sucker for a sob story. He's a proud dad and pictures of his children are blue tacked all over the walls, they regularly come to the house and he keeps their scooters and a few toys in his room. When he was broke he still remembered their birthdays, kitted them out from charity shops in an attempt to provide and made sure he never missed an access visit. He's now debt free, works hard and his kids are absolutely delightful - they've never stayed over for the night as Jason's mum lives nearby.

John: a great bloke, handsome, but unreliable and slightly hygienically challenged. Claimed his wife had him done for domestic abuse and kept moving so he couldn't make contact with her or their three children. He was with me for over a year until I had to evict him for non payment of rent, but we left on friendly terms and he'd managed to trace his children via Facebook. Domestic abuse? I doubt it, he visibly cowered when I had to give him my "I'm your New Best Friend before homelessness" talk.

Colin: has been with me for over 3 years and is in his mid twenties. He has a 9 year old son, Billy, who lives with the mother and her heroin addict boyfriend on a council estate. Colin tries hard, earns little and is a constant worrier - he also managed to get his new girlfriend pregnant earlier this year so he and I had to have a chat about "responsibility". Billy has been somewhat a victim of tug of love, as his mother decides as and when Colin can see him and it can be very irregular. Colin misses him when he's not allowed access (for no good reason), can't claim legal aid to challenge any access issues but showers Billy with fatherly love and discipline when he stays over, especially as he was under threat of a junior ASBO. By the way, Colin doesn't want to move in with his girlfriend as he's enjoying the house share so much and she has three other kids!

Neil: again, mid twenties and a bit of a wide boy with a beautiful three year old daughter. She used to stay over every other weekend until one my female meddling tenants suggested that the sleeping arrangements were "inappropriate".

She narrowly avoided a punch.

Tom: the saddest case of all. Two years ago his wife revealed that his 18 year old son wasn't actually his and to this day they still haven't spoken............

The Point I'm Trying To Make

HMOs are NOT a suitable environment for a child to grow up in, not least due to the transient and unreliable tenants but also because "Power Rangers" at 6 am on a Sunday morning could be classed as anti-social behaviour. However, who am I to say that a tenant can't have reasonable access to his child? He's lost everything and the only accommodation he can afford is a rented room in a shared house or a park bench. The bond between the parent and child should be allowed to grow during the difficult circumstances he's found himself in and it may just be the one thing that doesn't turn him to drink, drugs or beating up other tenants.

IMPORTANCE OF BEING A MEMBER OF A LANDLORD ASSOCIATION

However you decide to run your business, I can't stress enough the importance of being a member of a Landlord Association. Tenants can be canny and, before you've even finished the word "eviction" they will be sitting in the queue of the nearest Citizens Advice Bureau. Unless you are a property solicitor by profession, the law surrounding Assured Shorthold Tenancies can be tricky if the tenant wants to contest it. They can be badly behaved, dealing drugs, committing murder, stealing from little old ladies BUT THEY STILL HAVE TENANCY RIGHTS. Jail or dying in hospital does not mean the end of the tenancy! With a Landlord Association you have telephone access to fellow landlords who fully understand the law and can advise you, free of charge, forms and tenancy agreements, and the opportunity to attend meetings and network with other brave souls attempting to earn a crumb. (Actually, at our meetings I'm convinced they are all millionaires and I'm the only one hoping to register a profit before the next maintenance bill arrives).

Here's a list of some landlord associations:
National Landlords Association
www.landlords.org.uk
RLA: Residential Landlords Association
www.rla.org.uk
Scottish Association of Landlords
www.scottishlandlords.com
Landlord Law ***www.landlordlaw.co.uk***

There are some more regional ones, so use Google to find the right one for you.

HMOs AND THE LAW

I hate this bit. When we started I thought it was just a case of "give me the money and I'll pay the bills then cream a little bit of profit to go towards my next holiday". How wrong!

It has only been through trial and error, threatened court action against me, calls from Citizens Advice Bureau on behalf of tenants and a well known criminal telling ME his rights that I finally think I've nailed it. Doing a Landlord Accreditation Course is well worth the investment of time and will prevent you from inadvertently breaking the law and having a Tenant Relations Officer banging on your door.

Most councils have made their HMO regulations available on the Internet. This will cover the amount of bathrooms and kitchens per room (typically 1 bath, 1 toilet and 1 kitchen per 5 rooms), fire precautions and any other stipulations they require as well as whether or not they require you to licence the house and pay their fees (these are NOT standard across the country).

HOW TO DEAL WITH ANTISOCIAL BEHAVIOUR

Now the gritty bit. What happens when you have a tenant causing problems and how do you deal with it? If a tenant decides to be antisocial it immediately affects the other housemates and their safety. It's up to you, as a responsible landlord, to iron out these problems quickly and fairly before the other good tenants decide to leave or police take matters into their own hands. So, what constitutes antisocial behaviour?

Smoking

Smoking is not permitted inside ANY houses by law as it constitutes a shared area. If a tenant decides to lose a fag under the duvet whilst pissed and in no fit state to put out a fire, the entire house is affected and everyone will have to move out. Nicotine becomes embedded in the walls, curtains and carpets and, if there's enough smoke, will set off the smoke alarm in the room. Not a fun call out at midnight. Most fire brigades state the major cause of house fires is smoking.

Solution

I point out the error of their ways, explain the impact of a house fire and the fact it's not my responsibility to rehome them and, if they refuse to abide by the rule, ask them to leave via Section 21.

Noise

This can be subjective. One man's rock and roll is another man's headache; one may think it's OK to have rampant, noisy sex at midnight whilst the tenant below or next door finds it's interfering with his study of metaphysics, so the list goes on..... Whatever people may think of each other remind them that it's not OK to swear, write notes or abuse and intimidate other housemates. Despite your best efforts of judgement of personality, mistakes can happen and you may find your tenants incompatible.

Solution

Get the parties together and mediate what's acceptable and not acceptable. Try this out and, if they still can't agree, suggest that they may both be happier in another house.

Drugs

The bane of modern life and it's wise to operate a zero tolerance policy on any form of drug use except the occasional paracetamol or antibiotic. This isn't me passing judgement on how people spend their time but my experience has shown that weed DOES affect the brain and can make them paranoid. Also the practice tends to attract the type of unhinged and unpredictable people who the housemates don't really want to encounter on their way to the bathroom.

Solution:

From the very beginning of the tenancy, the tenant knows that I won't tolerate any form of drug use. If I have hard facts that drugs are being taken and, even if I'm told to "chill out,

Grandma", I tell them that I WILL report them to the police if it continues and ask them to leave via the Section 21 route.

Tenant's partner

A room for single occupancy is let to one person and one person alone. Whilst a tenant's sex life is none of my business, it becomes a problem if the girlfriend/boyfriend use the facilities regularly enough to annoy the paying housemates. You've reference checked and taken on the tenant, NOT their squeeze.

Solution

If they want to live together, I suggest they find somewhere suitable or apply for one of my double rooms when it becomes available. However, my experience is that a couple don't fit easily into a house of single people – something to do with domestic territory!

In extreme cases – police involvement

Hopefully, you'll know from your own experience the difference between tolerable and criminal behaviour. If in any doubt, talk to your local PCSO (Police Community Support Officer) who has been trained to deal with all types of antisocial behaviour and will have a list of solutions and outcomes up his or her sleeve. If it's an on-going problem such as noise or drugs, which is difficult for you to monitor out of working hours, ask them to keep an eye on the property.

If you can work with the police you're more likely to be able to negotiate a positive outcome as:

a) the tenant will get fed up with being the focus of attention and,

b) you'll be demonstrating to the other house-mates that you value their safety and right to quiet enjoyment of the property.

Bear in mind though that most tenants will be reluctant to give witness statements for an incident if there's a possibility of meeting the perpetrator on the way to the bathroom!

If the behaviour is criminal and causing distress, it's your job to get them to leave as quickly and legally as possible.

HOW TO ASK A TENANT TO LEAVE – LEGALLY!

If you've kept an eye on the house and already tried to address the problem through calm communication and presentation of the facts but the difficult tenant won't mend his ways, it's time to negotiate their departure. As stated before, it's important to remember that, regardless of their behaviour, tenants have rights and these must be borne in mind at all times during the eviction process.

If my tenant isn't abiding by the rules of the tenancy I offer them the following choice as to how to leave. The theory being that they've chosen to breach the tenancy conditions so it's only fair they choose how they wish to leave the property. Meet them in a communal space, such as the kitchen (not their room) and ask if they'd like to have a witness present and, if they do, get one for yourself to ensure objectivity. Discuss the problems that have arisen and any facts showing that it's that particular tenant causing the problems and then discuss the following options:

1. Give back their deposit, in cash, regardless of the state of the room if they will leave within an agreed time period which will depend on the risk of their behaviour to the other housemates – it's your call.

2. Explain to them that you will be serving a Section 21 notice (if this coincides with the end of the fixed term or is outside the fixed term) which will give them no less than 2 months or 8 weeks (depending on the frequency of due rent payments) and

their deposit may not be repaid if there is damage to the room. I will also ask the police to keep an eye on the property during their rounds in case of suspicious activity.

3. If the Section 21 notice is ignored, state that you will apply to the court for possession and, if necessary, bailiff involvement, apply for a CCJ (County Court Judgement) for any rent arrears and all court and bailiff fees will be payable by them. Going down this route will also mean it'll be nigh on impossible for them to secure rented accommodation in the future, as it will be very difficult to provide them with a good reference.

4. I haven't mentioned Section 8 notices (breach of contract within the fixed term) as these take too long to put into action and, if it's criminal behaviour, you'll need plenty of witness statements. It's quicker and cheaper to go for Option 1.

Now, if a tenant is or has been under a criminal investigation, even though these are civil laws, my experience has shown that they will want to avoid any court or official attention at all costs and are unlikely to have the money to repay CCJs, etc. It goes without saying that it's only Option 1 that will give them something with which to move on. Once you have a mutually agreeable outcome, ask for the return of the keys (which signifies the end of a tenancy) and a signed Voluntary Leaving (an example is at the back of this book) letter so you can't be accused of throwing them out!

WHAT TO DO WHEN A TENANT GOES AWOL (ABSENT WITHOUT LEAVE)?

There are two types of AWOL tenant:

1) They haven't been physically seen or heard of for over a month and owe rent.

2) They are living in the house but not talking to you

Type 1

In my tenancy agreements I have an additional clause that asks for tenants to let me know if they are going to be absent from the house for more than a week and to make sure that any rent due is paid in advance. This is so that I know their trip has been planned in advance and they're not lying in a gutter somewhere waiting to be identified.

Here is an example of additional clauses included in my tenancy agreements:

1. Tenant is responsible for own visitors in case of damage and noise.

2. Tenant cannot allow visitors to use the shower, cooker, washing machine, etc. in the premises. If visitors have to use them or stay overnight the landlord must be informed. There can only be a refusal or charge by the landlord (This clause is used to prevent a partner or friend moving into the property on a permanent basis and not to discourage an active social life.)

3. Tenant is responsible for taking out his/her own contents insurance for the room.

4. The tenant must inform the landlord if she/he is to be away from the premises for more than 1 week and pay the rent in advance accordingly.

I could make out that this is due to genuine concern for the tenants' welfare and it is – in part. However, I now back off and realise that it's their lives and they can live them/screw them up how they like, but experience has taught me that a room belonging to an AWOL tenant still has rights of tenancy slapped across it even if the rent's not being paid. What do you do?

First, don't assume that, just because the tenant has ceased paying rent and there's a pair of dirty pants and a couple of fag ends on the bed, that the room can be cleared and re-let. It could be that he only has 1 pair of pants and was saving the fag ends for a special occasion. In this case you have to go down the Abandonment Process (any landlord association can help) which involves taking a picture of the room, posting a notice on the door asking the tenant to get in touch and leaving things be for a month to see if you can elicit a response. Just make sure the room DOES look abandoned as if there's any chance that there is enough evidence to suggest your tenant is merely frugal and not paying you, you'll have to go down the repossession route of Section 21.

Type 2
What do you do if they're enjoying the facilities in the house but have decided to remove you from their contact list and are conveniently out when you call AND, worse of all, they've stopped paying rent. As soon as the tenant stops paying rent, Plan A kicks in:

1) Contact tenant by phone or letter if no joy speaking to them

2) Visit the room on following rent due date to see if double rent has been left (this does sometimes happen!)

3) If no response from letter, contact next of kin to check tenant is alive or if they've recently been in contact

4) Issue Section 21 and follow procedure

Once the above has been completed and all legal notices are in place, depending on the gravity of the situation I proceed to Plan B. If the tenant is being antisocial and making everyone in the house's lives hell then you can't sit behind legal notices and wait for the situation to play itself out, especially if other tenants are at risk.

In this situation, I fill up a bag with coffee, magazines, a good book and any sewing projects I have on the go and park myself outside the tenant's room until he comes home. I'm not harassing, just checking that the heating in the communal areas is working and investigating my other tenants' complaints of antisocial behaviour to take a view if the police should be involved or not.

As soon as said tenant thinks it's safe to come home, he saunters up the stairs and sees me – it's a look I wish I could capture time and time again! I invite him into the kitchen to have a chat and, luckily, he's too shocked to protest.
I then proceed to How To Ask A Tenant To Leave - Legally.

HOW FAR DO YOU LET A TENANT BUILD UP RENT ARREARS?

In the normal world of landlording and legally speaking, it's recommended to allow two months worth of arrears to build up before issuing any notices. However, this isn't normal landlording otherwise everyone would be doing it!

Every Saturday, my tenants hear my bailiff style knock on the door between 9.30 am and 11 am. I'm not so archaic that I don't offer for them to pay by standing order but only one tenant does this - I'm presuming the rest choose collection so the boys can show off their pants to me every week. If I've trained them well, they'll be clutching the cash as they open their door or, if they don't want to be disturbed, leave it in an envelope poking under the door.

So, what happens when they aren't proffering the week's rent? Again, if they remember their training they'll have called me a day or so beforehand with a suitable excuse to which I'll sound suitably empathetic whilst I wait for them to tell me how they'll sort the situation out and by what date. If they're too scared to talk to me or have conveniently forgotten they rent a room at the address, they'll go AWOL but that's a different subject which demands an alternative procedure which I made up but is fairly effective. Another time....! The great thing about HMOs is that if one room doesn't pay up the other rooms should be still covering the mortgage and bills so you can attend to the non payer without worrying about repossession or delving into your own bank account.

Liam - An Erratic Payer

Liam rents my bedsit in a licensable HMO. It's an attic room with it's own cooking facilities and he shares the bathroom with everyone else. He arrived on the doorstep two years ago - muscular, vertically challenged, bursting with testosterone, cheeky smile and looks rather attractive in his underpants (which I found out three weeks into the tenancy, it wasn't part of the referencing process!). Liam was a window fitter until the recession when events seemed to conspire against him. He's picked up a variety of jobs on building sites, shop work and anyone who'll have him but it's been fraught with contracts suddenly coming to an end, broken promises and his inability to manage money. He received a tax rebate earlier this year when he was £350 in arrears; I called him to discover he was on the bus to meet some friends "but don't worry it'll be there on Monday". Was it heck. He said his mates got him so drunk that he'd blown the lot at the casino - "I felt such a twat" he said. Yep, he said it, not me.

How far do you let someone go and how far do you believe the stories, show compassion, remember what it was like when you were young and rubbish with money? I'm now short on good-will after he phoned me on Sunday about the "stupid ****ing council won't give me housing benefit! What do they expect me to do? I'd wring their ****ing necks if I could get past the bullet proof glass!" It was my day off enjoying a bit of retail therapy and I so wasn't interested in another set of excuses .... and told him. "In that case" he said "I've got no other option but to do what my mates are doing and sell drugs but don't worry, I

won't do it while I'm at your house" Gee, thanks. However, I'm not worried for the existing street dealers just yet, as he has as much ability to blend into dark alleyways to do a deal with a junkie as a market trader advertising the catch of day.
I've given him a flexible payment schedule, bunged him a fiver when he had nothing to eat and no parents to call on (I'm such a sucker for orphans), a shoulder to cry on and offered cheaper rooms. I've made him sound like an arrogant idiot but he's lovely and I'm just annoyed that he hasn't sorted himself out and is trying to rile me with the drug threat.

What is Acceptable?
Nip the problem in the bud. If the tenant is late without good reason, serve a Section 21 notice for the end of the fixed term or 2 months/8 weeks if periodic. However explain that, providing the rent is brought up to date within this time period no further action will be taken, but it also means that you don't lose valuable weeks being strung along with another set of excuses. A Section 21 notice can be withdrawn by you.

Rent Statements:
If your tenant is over a week late or is paying sporadically, give him/her a rent statement every time they make a payment so you both know where you stand. Mine look not unlike bank statements:

A N Other Rent Statement
as at 8th January 2012
Tenant paying 1 week in advance

Date Due	Amount Due	Amount Received	Balance
18/09/2011	£80.00	£80.00	£0.00
25/09/2011	£80.00	£0.00	-£80.00
02/10/2011	£80.00	£0.00	-£160.00
09/10/2011	£80.00	£0.00	-£240.00
16/10/2011	£80.00	£0.00	-£320.00
23/10/2011	£80.00	£0.00	-£400.00
30/10/2011	£80.00	£0.00	-£480.00
06/11/2011	£80.00	£0.00	-£560.00
13/11/2011	£80.00	£0.00	-£640.00
17/11/2011		£200.00	-£440.00
20/11/2011	£80.00	£0.00	-£520.00
27/11/2011	£80.00	£0.00	-£600.00
01/12/2011		£140.00	-£460.00
04/12/2011	£80.00	£0.00	-£540.00
11/12/2011	£80.00	£0.00	-£620.00
18/12/2011	£80.00	£0.00	-£700.00
19/12/2011		£200.00	-£500.00
26/12/2011	£80.00	£0.00	-£580.00
01/01/2012	£80.00		-£660.00

Yes, he left owing £660 after pocketing his Local Housing Allowance.

Local Housing Allowance Arrears

If a tenant is receiving LHA/Housing Benefit and is 8 weeks or more in arrears, you can apply to your local Housing department, enclosing proof of arrears such as the statement above and copies of LETTERS (not texts) to prove that you have been actively chasing the money.

Conclusion

You will suffer from rent arrears and, rather than throwing good money after bad, accept your losses (which can be offset against tax), refurbish the room and move on. Please don't take a baseball bat to your tenant – the whole beauty of HMOs is still being able to pay the mortgage and utility bills if only 4 out of 5 rooms are up to date on their rent.

It IS possible to make money AND be compassionate when dealing with HMO tenants - the two are not mutually exclusive. I make my entry level costs to a room affordable i.e. £150 deposit plus one week's rent in advance, unlike other landlords who demand one month's rent and one month's deposit in advance - now that's a lot of money.

WHAT HAPPENS WHEN A TENANT DIES?

At some point in your career as a Landlord you'll encounter all aspects of the human lifecycle: birth, toddlers, teenagers, retired and dying or death. Tenants don't hand in their notice, clean up, move out and THEN expire.

Here are two posts from my blog covering the subject of how I tried to find out if my tenant was still alive – and what happens when you face your tenants' demise from this world:

A Moral Dilemma – Is My Tenant Still Alive? Where's Steve?
Six weeks have now passed since I've had any contact with Steve. He was the tenant in one of my largest rooms priced at £100 pw including all bills but, as he'd stopped smoking weed in the house and I thought we'd come to a mutual understanding on how to behave, I gave him a preferential rate of £90 pw. Why? Because I still hadn't learnt from the old adage "Give 'em and inch and they'll take a mile".

After a marijuana incident (i.e. the whole street was mellowing under its influence, the smell was so strong) and he'd asked to move into the bigger room, we got on well. Housing Benefit paid his LHA allowance direct to me because Steve had been/still is a gambling addict and he then paid as a top up. He's now 2 months down on his top up and nobody has heard sight nor sound of him. His post is still there, his pants are still in the drawer, some toiletries are still on the dresser and his bed looks like, well, any man's bed who isn't hoping to impress a girl. I've written to his guarantor and tried to contact his mother with no success.

From a legal point of view, because he'd moved room but within the same property, I'd created a new tenancy which meant I had to serve Section 21 notice for the end of his fixed term of the expiry date. I was a bit annoyed as I'd received two legal viewpoints at the time from a landlord association. One told me to just get him to sign a letter acknowledging the move to a new room but it would continue as a periodic tenancy. Another member of the team told me to create to a new fixed term agreement and re-register the deposit. Confusing, but all paperwork has been sorted, served and is now strewn across his bed presumably in case he runs out of toilet roll.

Moral Dilemma

So, I'm in a dilemma. House is quiet and stable without him, I'm getting two thirds of his rent paid direct to me by the council and I don't have the expense of refurbishing his room which is likely to cost £200 (new carpet and full paint). Do I consider the room to be abandoned (but I think there are slightly too many belongings, albeit they've been undisturbed for six weeks); or proceed to get a court order if he hasn't moved the stuff out by 14th December? Morally, I probably should be trying harder to find him as we're a small town and people don't just disappear, but his phone's ringing so he's clearly still charging it. I do worry, with his history, that he could have come to a sticky end, but hope a relative would've wanted to lay claim to his paltry belongings. However, I haven't applied for a court order before, so I'd like to be able to say I know how to do it. What would you do?

DEATH OF A TENANT – LITERALLY

I've just returned from the funeral of a tenant who rented a room from me 18 months ago and although his story is sad, it's not uncommon. Before I went, I was going to write a jokey blog about tenants dying on you but now, possibly sobered by seeing his coffin, I'm hoping to approach this subject sensitively.

Duncan

Duncan came to me after a friend begged me to give him a home as he'd suffered alcohol addiction for years and was moving to our town to start afresh. His sister in law found him a job and accommodation, and he seemed resigned to the plans made for him. Six months later, after a drunken full-on fight with another tenant at 2 am (a fire alarm had been set off) he decided to progress to a one bed flat - helped out financially by his family. On moving day, I found him in bed with a girl he'd met the night before, completely unaware it was move out day and, returning at 6 pm that Saturday night, he was confused and couldn't remember where he'd left the car. The following day I sought help from his family only to be told "it's your problem". Kid gloves were removed and we had a man to man talk. A year on and despite rehab and great accommodation paid for by his family last week, he had a heart attack at 44 years old - too young.

Harry
Now, I'm proud to say that I haven't had a tenant die under one of my roofs, yet. Last year I housed another alcoholic (didn't know it at the time) and, as the year progressed it became clear he was very ill. I got a text from his housemate to say she'd had to call an ambulance for him at 3 am but no one knew what had happened and could I check up? I contacted the hospital and discovered him in MAU (Medical Assessment Unit) and visited. Looking frail, he said he'd been in touch with his next of kin and could I find him some personal items from his room. "Oh, sorry, it's a bit of a mess". THAT was an understatement, but being charitable kind of girls, Nicky (the housemate) and I tackled his room with Marigolds and disinfectant as he'd clearly been living in his own mess for weeks. We sorted out the bed, bought clean sheets, pjs, etc. from the charity shop and I went to see him again clutching new toothbrush and pants from Primark. Surprised not to find any relatives had been, the nurse sent him home with me in hospital issue pjs. We sat in the car park, both feeling that the professional bridge of landlord/tenant had been crossed and I simply didn't know what to do with him as he stunk, was frail and just wanted to get home.

Two months later and the calls started again to say that the toilet was filthy and he hadn't been seen. When I visited him to collect his rent it was clear that he was desperately unwell but wouldn't phone his next of kin and said he'd "sort it out". I'm not medically trained, but even I could see his body couldn't hold out much longer, so contacted Adult Social Services. They were just fantastic and visited him with me and tried in vain to get him the help he needed as his organs were slowly shutting down due to alcohol. By the time the ambulance was called we learnt that he was an alcoholic drowning out the pain of Crohn's disease and failed marriages. As he was wheeled off he did the decent thing and gave me his rent for the month. Three days later the hospital asked me to come in at 6.30 am. Several cups of tea and "we're doing everything we can" later I realised that he'd made me next of kin and I was watching a dying man take his last breaths. The responsibility was too great to bear so, ignoring his wishes, I contacted his daughter - the family had to have the choice whether or not to see him. They came to the hospital and he was just coherent enough to let go of my hand and register relief at seeing his children. Two hours later he died and the family called me with the news - there is no place to hide in a school playground while you're sobbing your heart out.

The housemates and I were all gracefully invited to the funeral and listened to what a wonderful man he had been - London firefighter, father, husband, keen gardener. Lots of family and friends turned up to honour his name and yet he hadn't had a single visitor at the house in all those months and had lost so many mobiles. The embarrassment on their faces when they found out that we had prevented his having an inhumane, lonely death in a rented room was palpable.

After taking the house back this year for my family to live in, his bedroom is now my bedroom. I thought it would be creepy and unsettling after seeing the state of it and watching his children's disgust as they went through his belongings. It's been completely gutted and I feel completely at peace with his spirit.

I have another near death experience to tell you but have decided to deliver that story another time with the light-heartedness it deserves, as the tenant is still alive and making the lives of those in contact with him hell!

So, Harry and Duncan. RIP to you both and I hope your demons have now been chased away. This is one landlady who would like to have done more.

Legally Speaking
Be very aware that if your tenant dies during his/her Assured Shorthold Tenancy, the tenancy passes to the next of kin or deceased's estate. Luckily, none of Harry's family wanted to rent a room.

WHAT MAKES AN HMO SUCCESSFUL?

After asking the tenants their opinion on what makes an HMO a happy, harmonious place to live they all said the following:

1. Leave each other alone and mind your own business
2. Respect for privacy and quiet
3. Adhere to the Rules of the House
4. Ability to sort own problems out and not inflict them on housemates
5. Keep antisocial behaviour away from the house
6. When in the kitchen, make a cuppa for each other

ELECTRICAL TESTS AND FIRE SYSTEMS

A very quick word about this as it's important from a safety point of view and keeping your HMO licence. Check with your local council what electrical certificates they expect (electrical safety test is every 5 years) and with your electrician about PAT (Portable Appliance Testing) which should be done on shared items such as microwaves, kettles, irons, vacuum cleaner, washing machine, etc. annually.

Go to ***www.pat-testing.info*** for more information.

HOW NOT TO BECOME A ROGUE LANDLORD!

- Treat your tenants as you expect to be treated yourself
- Do keep the property in good condition and damp free
- Don't try to dodge the rules, there's no point. Your council officer has enough Rogue Landlords on his books and the power to prosecute
- It's not all about making money and yields, it's about providing safe accommodation for PEOPLE
- There's a Housing Law just as there are lots of other laws, IGNORANCE IS NO DEFENCE!

On that note I shall refer you to the words of Ben Reeve-Lewis, who has written probably the first easy to read overview of the Housing Law and how it applies to you.

I hope you're still feeling positive about investing in HMOs. If you start out as you mean to go on they can be educational, interesting, give you plenty of customers/tenants and a profitable business model. If you have any questions at all please contact me at:

hmolandlady@hotmail.co.uk.

A Concise and Important Guide to Housing Law

– By Ben Reeve-Lewis

Ben negotiates in disputes between landlords and tenants, is a housing law trainer and consultant, property journalist and occasional broadcaster ***(benreevelewis@yahoo.co.uk)***

Of course it isn't all fun being an HMO landlord. Much heartache, cost and hassle is endured by landlords unnecessarily, all because so many fail to understand one single thing. Would you like to know what that single thing is?

It is this.

The minute you hand over the keys to a tiny box room, you are in the same legal position as a council with 10,000 properties to manage.

The Housing Law Encyclopaedia is 2 feet thick and weighs in at 26 lbs, I know, I have stuck it on bathroom scales. In many instances when the landlord gets the laws wrong, it's a criminal offence, not just a civil one.

Misunderstanding the laws that relate to lettings can cost a landlord a fortune and tie them up in all sorts of legislation and regulation that they wish they had never started.

There are around 17 different legal types of contract through which people can occupy property. All of them have their own rules and procedure and some differ widely from each other. If you get the paperwork or procedure wrong, it can cost a fortune and a lot of time and annoyance.

This bit of your Sussed book will give you a brief overview of the basics. It doesn't go into too much detail, it would bore you to tears, but I do aim to address some of the common misunderstandings in a little bit of detail.

Tenancy or Licence?

There are 2 basic ways that an occupier can, er.....occupy!

- As a tenant, or
- As a licensee

The important thing to know is you, the landlord, don't get to choose which type they are. Whether they hold a tenancy or a licence in law is determined by such things as the type of building they are in, where the landlord lives, the date they moved in, whether meals are cooked for them etc.

Writing the word 'Licence' on top of an occupation agreement doesn't make them a licensee.

A tenancy is a legal asset capable of transfer to another, which is why people can inherit council tenancies and carry out mutual exchanges.

A licence of any kind, is not capable of transfer and is, in effect, only permission to occupy – needing only withdrawal of that permission to end the person's legal rights.

This is why a landlord cannot choose which type of occupancy they want to grant. Many landlords would make all their residents licensees and simply tell them to go when they hit a problem.

It doesn't work like that.

The defining case law on this issue is Street v. Mountford 1986, where Judge Templeman had to decide whether a case before him was a licence agreement or a tenancy agreement.

He famously said:
"The manufacture of a 5 pronged implement for manual digging results in a fork, even if the manufacturer, unfamiliar with the English language, claims to have made a spade".

So there you go.

Tenancy Agreements

Believe it or not you don't have to issue a written tenancy agreement to create a tenancy, and not having a written agreement doesn't mean that the tenant has no legal rights.

As we saw earlier it is the factual circumstances that surround the letting that determine what type of tenant or licensee the person actually is.

Going back to the Street v Mountford case, Judge Templeman identified 3 hallmarks of a tenancy:

- Rent or service must be due
- For a clear term (for instance weekly rent)
- The occupier must have exclusive use of their accommodation.

In other words, as long as they have at least 1 room that they rent and don't have to share with anyone who isn't part of their family (for instance a couple sharing), and have the right to exclude anyone from their accommodation, then it will be a tenancy not a licence.

Then it is simply the type of tenancy that is at issue, and that is determined by things like the status of the landlord (council, housing association, private) and the date that the tenancy began.

As we saw before, it isn't just about Assured Shorthold Tenancies. There are many different types as with tenancies and licences. Putting 'Assured Shorthold Tenancy' on the contract doesn't necessarily make it one.

Fortunately the vast majority of tenancies in the private sector are ASTs these days, so don't worry too much.

Tenancy Clauses

You can add any clause you like to a letting agreement, but bear in mind that even if the tenant has signed it and subsequently breaches a clause, it doesn't automatically mean that you could enforce it legally.

A clause must be reasonable and fair to be enforceable, and take into account that the occupier has the right to use the property in what is called a 'Tenant-Like manner'.

I have regularly seen clauses in HMO agreements insisting that a person isn't allowed any overnight guests. It is a perfectly 'Tenant-Like' thing to have a guest stay over. Any landlord would have a serious problem trying to evict for this. However if that guest causes nuisance or annoyance to the other residents, then that would be a valid breach, because tenants are responsible for the behaviour of their guests.

It's important not to confuse these 2 issues as one could give you the possession order you seek while the other could lose your case for you.

The Office of Fair Trading has guidance notes on unfair terms in residential lettings contracts. A free PDF can be found here ***http://www.oft.gov.uk/shared_oft/reports/unfair_contract_terms/oft356.pdf***

Visits and access to the property

Remember that as tenants the occupiers have exclusive occupation of their property, which includes the right to exclude anyone they like, including the landlord.

Normal procedure when a landlord wants to access a person's accommodation, for instance to carry out inspections or repairs, is to give the tenant 24 hours notice in writing of their intention. The tenant shouldn't unreasonably withhold permission.

However, the time or date that you want to do your visit may not fit in with your tenant's plans, and many tenants don't want people in their accommodation when they aren't there themselves. So be prepared for a bit of flexibility on this one.

If a tenant steadfastly refuses to allow access and you need to do a repair, you can go to court and obtain a thing called an Interim Possession Order, an IPO, which is a kind of injunction, a court order telling the tenant to let you in. And don't forget, if it is a repair issue and damage occurs as a result of the tenants refusal, you can withhold money from their deposit and also charge them the court fee for obtaining the IPO. It is worth mentioning this when discussing access with an unhelpful tenant.

Of course as an HMO landlord your property will mainly consist of individual bed-sits. The tenants have exclusive use of their rooms but the rest of the house is regarded as 'Common parts'.
A landlord doesn't need permission to be in those areas.

The dreaded eviction procedure

You have probably all heard of this. How costly and time consuming it all is, and also how sometimes completely pointless it turns out to be.

I won't lie to you, it is all of those things, but if you don't follow the procedure, however arcane and downright mad it seems, you could find that you have committed a criminal offence and get sued by your tenant and the council at the same time.

Laws and procedures on the eviction process are very complex and important to get right. Don't rely on this brief introduction to be enough information to enable you to do it. You can do it yourself but you can also pay a solicitor or one of a number of online specialist eviction services.

There are 3 main bits to it:

- Serve a notice
- Get a possession order
- Go back to court and get a warrant

Serve a notice

My job here is to simply let you know the legal side of things, not to make you feel any better about it. As you may be beginning to gather now, housing law is far from simple but it does apply to you.

There are many different types of notice that pertain to different types of tenancy. Get the wrong notice or fill it in wrong and like snakes and ladders, when you finally get to court you find yourself slipping all the way back to the start.

Understand this single point though:

A notice is only that. It puts the tenant 'On-Notice' that you are intending to seek possession of the property. The notice is only stage 1; it does not end the tenant's right to occupy on its own.

It will run for a set period of time - from 2 weeks to 2 months depending on the type of notice it is - and the reason that possession is being sought. ONLY AFTER the notice period has expired can the landlord apply to court for the possession order.

Get a Possession Order

There are different types of possession order and for all you private landlords, 17 different Grounds for eviction, at least one of which must be proven to the judge's satisfaction before they will grant possession.

For some grounds, like nuisance (Ground 14) or some rent arrears (Grounds 10 and 11) even if you prove it the judge could still only grant a Suspended Possession Order, which means you haven't got rid of your tenant, only got a court order that will allow you to go back in the future.

This is because courts take the loss of a home very seriously and only do it when they have no other choice.

Accelerated Proceedings

Of course most landlords these days know the difficulties of seeking possession using the 17 Grounds and choose instead to evict the tenant simply because the fixed term of their original agreement has expired.

You don't have to prove any of the 17 Grounds to do this. In fact whatever you do, don't put rent arrears or nuisance on you paperwork, it will really muck things up.

The courts have a special procedure for this, the Accelerated Procedure. It is recognised that a tenant has no defence to these types of claim and the procedure avoids the need for a court appearance, the possession order simply comes out in the post.

Go back to court and get a warrant

Many landlords make the costly mistake of thinking that once they have the possession order they can simply change the locks.

If you do that you will have breached Section 1 of the Protection from Eviction Act 1977 and committed a criminal offence.

If the tenant doesn't move out when the date for possession expires, the landlord must go back to court and obtain a Warrant of Eviction. Only when the locks have been changed by your locksmith supervised by the court bailiffs will you have your property back lawfully.

Of course if a tenant leaves at any time during this procedure you don't have to carry on with any further legal action, but you will need to be damn sure they have gone and aren't simply away visiting friends or staying at Her Majesty's Pleasure.

Which leads us neatly to.....

The law on abandonment

This is a very common legal headache for HMO landlords because a high proportion of HMO tenants often come with drink, drug and mental health issues, leading them to live what we in the housing world politely call "Chaotic lifestyles". Their living patterns can be unpredictable and stable connections with friends or family may not be that regular.

Basically you can't consider a property officially abandoned if there is any 'evidence of an intention to return', that could include scraps of clothes or toiletries in the bathroom.

Even if other residents tell you they have definitely gone, tread carefully. It can be prudent to still follow the eviction procedure so that there are no come-backs if the tenant returns unannounced and accuses you of having illegally evicted them.

Here is an example of how complex this can get. In Hackney v. Ampratum 2003, a Ghanaian woman was deported for breaching immigration status. Her children stayed with her ex-partner in what was their council home. The council sought possession saying she had surrendered the property by being deported but the judge over-ruled this argument, stating that the fact that the children were still there was evidence of 'an expectation to return', even though she had no control over when or if it would happen.

This is the kind of world you are in, messy and very, very legalistic.

Abandoned Goods

Often a tenant will have left the property, presuming you have strong evidence they have abandoned, for instance, they wrote you a note and pushed the keys through your letterbox, but still, left belongings in there.

'Not my problem' you find yourself saying. WRONG!!!! Slide back down the snake, do not pass go, do not collect £200. There is a little thing called the Torts (Interference with Goods) Act 1977 to deal with. The Act is here: ***http://www.legislation.gov.uk/ukpga/1977/32***

As unfair as it may seem, a landlord does have a legal duty to personal effects left with them, you can't just dump them.

The Act requires you to make reasonable efforts to contact the tenant warning them that the goods need collecting.

It can be a really sensible idea to get the tenant to provide a name and contact details of someone responsible for this when they sign up for the tenancy. Then you know exactly who to go to. If they don't have anyone, you can place a small ad in a local paper advising that goods will be disposed of.

You need to give a reasonable period of time to allow them to collect their things. The legislation itself states 3 months is a reasonable period, but you could add a clause to the tenancy agreement stating 14 days will be the period and that is usually enough.

If you can trace the tenant, then you have to serve a formal notice on them with a date for action, after which you can sell or dispose.

If goods are sold, the landlord is allowed to keep back money for reasonable sale and remuneration. Any money left over is to be held for the tenant for up to 6 years.

Surrender and Termination

Tenants can of course lawfully end their tenancy. There are 2 ways to do this:

- Termination
- Surrender

Termination

A tenancy is terminated by the tenant giving a month's notice in writing that they will be leaving. The problem here is if they change their minds and stay. A landlord still can't use force to evict them, they will have to follow a court procedure, which is lengthy and expensive. The costs of action can charged to the tenant, but it doesn't mean you will get the money.

Believe it or not there is an obscure piece of legislation that for once can help. It is called the Distress for Rent Act 1737, which can be found here:
http://www.legislation.gov.uk/apgb/Geo2/11/1977/32

This old law allows a landlord to charge a tenant double the rent on a daily basis for every day they remain in the property after having terminated their agreement.

I often find mentioning this fact to tenants can help them make quick decisions.

Surrender

This is where the tenant actually surrenders by acting a certain way rather than terminating in writing. The law on surrender states there must be an "unequivocal act of surrender and also an unequivocal act of acceptance on behalf of the landlord".

Typically that would be the tenant giving the keys to the landlord, who gives him a receipt saying "Ta very mooch".

Be careful of 'implied surrender' – in other words, don't presume a property has been surrendered. Case law is many and varied on this matter, just like abandonment.

Landlord Harassment

Obviously as a landlord you want to avoid any allegations of harassment being thrown your way and I'm sure you wouldn't ever consider yourself to be the type of landlord who harasses their tenants. However harassment is defined in law and just because you don't think you have harassed your tenant it doesn't mean that the law would agree with you.

I have prosecuted many landlords who, even when being fined by the judge, shake their head and cannot see why what they have done would be considered harassment.

This is because harassment is when you threaten or assault your tenant right? WRONG!!!!! Slide back down the snake, do not pass go etc. etc.

Harassment of residential occupiers is defined slightly differently in different laws but basically it can best be described as:

"Acts that are done that are likely to cause the residential occupier to give up their premises".

Harassment is more easily understood when you see it from the perspective of the 'likely' results of the actions, not the actual intentions of the landlord.

For instance, a tenant hasn't paid you any rent for 2 months. They don't answer their phone when you call and despite many promises never come good, and you see them down the betting shop every day.

It is reasonable to keep calling the tenant about it, after all its money they owe you. It's also reasonable to knock on their door when they get home in the evening isn't it?

Section 40 of the Administration of Justices Act 1970 makes it a criminal offence for a person to: "Harasses the other with demands for payment which by their frequency, or the manner or occasion of their making, or any accompanying threat or publicity are calculated to subject him or his family or household to alarm, distress or humiliation".

You see? It's about the likely effect of the action, not the landlord's intention.

So many landlords fall foul of harassment accusations without ever intending to.

Prosecution for harassment

There are 2 arms to this. There is the criminal prosecution under the Protection from Eviction Act 1977 and related legislation, and there is the civil version of it which is called "Breach of Covenant for Quiet Enjoyment".

The council prosecutes the criminal offences. These cases take an age to get through court and most councils will only do it where the allegations are very serious, for instance where violence was used. Most cases end up with a fine and some with imprisonment.

Tenants can take out civil claims though, which are dealt with far more quickly and come with high levels of damages, often in the tens of thousands of pounds.

Many disputes arise between landlords and tenants and the vast majority come to naught. The best way to resolve them is to sit down and chat with the tenants, build a good relationship with them. When parties do get into dispute many areas have mediation services that can help. Even the council's housing advice teams can sometimes be of use.

However if a tenant is intent on making an accusation, be up front with anyone who contacts you on their behalf. Don't react to the affront you feel by the accusations, it goes down far better with investigating officers for the council if the landlord is being reasonable.

Repairs

Most tenancy agreements contain clauses saying the tenants are responsible for keeping drains and gutters clean etc., however there are some repairs that will always be the legal duty of the landlord. They are covered by Section 11 of the Landlord and Tenant Act 1985.

The landlord is responsible for carrying out any repairs to the structure of the building, so we are talking walls, roof, doors, floors etc., also for the repair of fixed utilities such as water and gas and the appliances that were supplied to use them, like cookers and boilers.

Landlords are not obliged to fix free standing heaters.

I often find broken windows cause a lot of problems in HMOs. Technically speaking they are part of the structure and therefore the landlord's responsibility but if the tenant has broken one then a certain amount of two-way bargaining needs to go on, which admittedly might not go well, but that's landlording for you. If it was all plain sailing where would the fun be?

A common question I get asked is "Can I withhold my rent if the landlord isn't doing the repairs?" The answer is they can, but it isn't just as simple as not paying you. It is called "right of set off", in other words the right to offset rent against outstanding repairs.

It should really be used where the landlord is completely failing or refusing to do a repair. The tenant needs to put the landlord on written notice that they will be doing so and then get quotes for the works to be done which should then be produced to the landlord. Only if the work remains outstanding should they then pay for it and withhold it from the rent.

To be honest, when a tenant asks me about this I tell them how it works but always suggest they think twice before doing it, as it can lead to messy rent arrears claims that might not go their way.

Conclusion

So there you go, a brief romp through some of the legal situations as they commonly occur in HMO lettings. As I said at the start of this piece this is just a very brief overview. The housing law case book alone runs to 1,200 pages and contains around 15,000 case laws and that doesn't include:

The Housing Act 1996

The Landlord and Tenant Act 1985

The Landlord and Tenant Act 1987

The Housing Act 1988

The Protection from Eviction Act 1977

The Rent Act 1977

The Housing Act 1985

The Housing Act 2004

And that's just to name but a few, all of which relate to landlord and tenant law.

It really is important for your mental health to understand that you cannot become a landlord casually, it is a serious legal business, not simply about renting out some space you have and raking in the cash.

You can be a landlord for 20 years and never have a major problem and then one nightmare tenant throws you into a world of expensive legislation

Also laws change regularly, particularly case laws, many new ones come through every single month.

Voluntary Leaving Letter

Note: It's advisable to have a copy of this ready for when you meet your tenant. Don't type in the date when preparing it. You can fill that in by hand when you're sure the tenant is ready to leave.

Date:

[Room Number]
[Full Address of Property to be vacated]

WITHOUT PREJUDICE

Dear [Landlord – insert your name]

I am voluntarily leaving the above room at the above address and surrender my tenancy agreement and all claim on the property.

Yours sincerely

A N Other
[Tenant's full name as it appears on the tenancy agreement]

TENANT INFORMATION FORM

First Name

Middle Name/s:

Surname (Block Capitals):

Date Of Birth:

Mobile Number:

Email:

Current Address:

Dates:

Name of Landlord:

Contact:

If less than 1 year, please supply previous address:

Dates:

NEXT OF KIN Relationship:

Name:

Address:

Home Tel No:

Mobile:

EMPLOYER: Position:

Company:

Supervisor:

Contact:

Deposit Details: Alternative address for the selected Deposit Scheme:

Alternative address:

Postcode/Country:

Do you smoke? Yes/No

Do you have any unspent criminal convictions? Yes/No

Detail:

Are you or will you be in receipt of Housing Benefit? Yes/No

Photographic evidence of identity:
(Passport/driving licence/student card)

Passport Number:

Driving Licence Number:

I declare that the information given by me is true and I hereby give the landlord/agent permission to use this information to carry out a search with a licensed credit reference agency.

Signed:

Date:

Go to my blog and get up-to-date:

http://hmolandlady.wordpress.com

THE "EASTER BREAK IN" POST

Happy Easter to all and I hope you've had a good break. I spent the holiday in Sweden without children and had the unique experience of sampling Elk meatballs, Swedish Easter pop then falling asleep in a posh garden shed by the lake in -5°C with no toilet. By happy chance, I'd managed to lose my mobile just before leaving the UK and reckoned that my HMO world could survive without me for three days and thank goodness I did leave it behind.............

Burglary – An Inside Job?

On my return one of my tenants, Jason, had used his initiative and found my home number which is posted on the communal notice boards after I failed to respond to any of his numerous texts and calls at 1 am on Saturday morning. He'd been pounding the streets all day selling key rings on behalf of a creative businessman in the guise of a charity (which I won't go into as I'm sure it's legitimate if questionably moral). As manager of the "gang" he'd taken £1,300 worth of takings back to his room and then gone out for the evening, got back in the early hours of Saturday to find his door had been smashed in, the cash taken but Playstation, laptop, etc. left well alone. Neither the front nor back doors had been forced so it became a foregone conclusion that it had been an inside job.

Now, my lot tend to act before they think and throw their weight around, accusing the person who looks the most scared or is not there to defend themselves. As it was the long Easter weekend most of the other tenants were either visiting their families or working extra hours, but Jason and the police managed to track down and establish everyone's whereabouts apart from Greg in the bedsit. By the time I returned on Monday morning, Jason had gathered fictional evidence, tried and sentenced Greg for the pure reason that he had disappeared for four days (as it turned out he was visiting his children and got lucky with an ex), reported his suspicions to the "Big Boss" who phoned me to ask for Greg's personal information which I refused to give.

Meeting the Local Gangster

The problem when you're dealing with people when they're emotional and suspicious is that they're just not thinking straight and nothing you say will appease them. Later that morning I visited the house myself to check out the damage and try to get a measure of the situation. Before I knew it, Andrew had opened the front door and three men burst up the stairs toward the bedsit stopping when they saw me, started smoothing their hair and pretended they'd popped in to check out the landing carpet. I asked what they were doing and they said they "just wanted a word" with Greg and to "ask him a few questions". I pointed out that subtlety wasn't their strong point and suggested we continue the discussion in the kitchen (mainly for my safety as the communal lights kept going out). The Boss (short stature, hard eyes, well dressed) wanted details of everyone in the house and how he "was going to get his money back" whilst his associates/flunkies shifted from one foot to the other, snarling and refusing to take their hoods off.

Intimidated? Me?

To be honest, I was a bit worried/annoyed and explained that if they wanted to "interview" all the tenants they could do so OUTSIDE the house and I considered it very rude that they barged in with no evidence to talk to people they'd never met. These were my tenants, my house and my bloody rules and if anyone is going to throw their weight around, it's me. Eventually, the Boss said "I ain't wasting my time here, we're off. It's not about the money, it's the principle and I want someone to pay". I kind of understand where he's coming from but also pointed out that the only person in the house who knew that money was there is a self confessed gambling addict (who also works for him), could be placed at the scene of the crime and was probably also stupid enough not to have either (a) broken down the other room doors so Jason's room wasn't singled out, (b) forced entry via the front door to look like an outside job or (c) open the house front door to the Boss and allow him and his boys to run amok unaccompanied.

What Now?

So, here I am with a house full of unhappy tenants, ready to throw a punch at anyone who dares to accuse any one of them. Jason has narrowed the culprit down now to Andrew but there's no hard evidence and I'm left with not just a room door to mend but also tenant trust – not easy when the likely perpetrator is still in situ.

If you feel sorry for them, think about this poor fella!

On a lighter note: whilst getting ready for the new term I found my son swinging his lunchbox around the kitchen and talking to it. A few minutes later, he appeared in tears saying that the zip had broken and he needed to open it quickly. Cursing cheap products, I went to chuck it in the bin and realised that there was something inside so cut the lid off only to find a very scared, sick looking guinea pig! We turned the lunchbox upside down, cut out a door and called it "home".

"THE BREAK-IN" RELOADED - My Follow-up Post

OK, so those of you who read my last post "Easter Break In" will know that an HMO room suffered a burglary where only cash was stolen (all other valuables left intact, including four bottles of champagne which proves it wasn't me as I would have nicked the champagne first). After discussions with the victim and the other tenants, who are quick to deny culpability, the badge of suspicion was laid on Andrew. I've since found out that he's not only a self confessed gambling addict, but is also on Pub Watch (this means he's been banned from every pub in town for punching someone) and is on probation doing community service for holding up a bookies (not sure what with though).

I've been mulling over a solution to this problem as:

a) There's no evidence it was him

b) The tenants are known by everyone in town that they repeatedly forget to lock the back door

c) I actually like the guy, he's paid his rent bang on time every week and is adamant he's innocent.

Watching My Move

In the meantime, I've got five other tenants watching what I'm going to do about it – one of whom is never there and only uses the room to store his stuff following his bankruptcy, another who is at work all day, a Romanian ex-border guard working for a hotel, Tom the alcoholic when he's got cash – salt of the earth when sober and the victim – a guy who is Andrew's manager and recommended him for a room in the first place. They've all been quick to lay the blame and "threaten to punch the first f****r" to put a foot wrong but shy away from any confrontation when I try to bring them all together to find a solution considering their suspicions are based on little more than reputation. And, to be honest, I have no idea who it was either.

The trouble is, as landlady, I have to be seen as impartial, fair, law abiding and on every tenant's side. These tenants, either through their own making or circumstances into which they are born, carry their vulnerabilities around with them until being defensive becomes a means of communication and, before I've even opened my mouth, assume what I'm going to say or interpret what I am saying as a personal attack on them.

The Solution

I had decided to tell Andrew that I wouldn't let his contract turn into a periodic at the end of his fixed term in July. Whilst the Section 21 would be a no fault notice, I felt that everyone was gunning for him, tensions were high and it would be better for all concerned if he found alternative accommodation. In fact, I have a room coming available that would suit him perfectly then, at least if anything else happened in the house, he couldn't be blamed for it.

Before I'd even started the car engine the "Big Boss" was on the phone to me pleading, yes, pleading for me to let him stay in a call that lasted 28 minutes. This was weird because I'd heard that even he thought Andrew had committed the crime and was waiting for him to mess up again and he wanted to know why was I "chucking him out?". I let him rant for a bit before explaining that I felt I was playing fair and then threw back to him – What would he do in my position? Wait for the inevitable showing of fists (note: showing NOT using), arguing and then everyone phoning me at midnight in the mistaken belief that I'm the police and can break up five grown men (two of whom are bound to be pissed)?

I left it with him that moving to another house may calm everyone down and allow Andrew to lead his life without preconceptions from fellow tenants; he suggested that I install CCTV cameras and security grilles. No to the grilles but last year I had been thinking about CCTV in the communal areas even though I really, really don't want to see tenants in their pants going to the bathroom.

Whilst I check out CCTV costs, anyone got any other ideas? Or the number for the United Nations?!

TOP 10 THINGS THAT WILL HAPPEN WHEN YOU OWN AN HMO

Once you are the proud owner of your fully tenanted HMO, these are things you can guarantee will happen:

1. No-one will admit to breaking the toilet seat/shower hose/shower door. However, it will be everyone else's fault.

2. Crockery, cutlery and glasses will disappear as quickly as you replace them - this can be blamed on the fictitious elves that are equipping their new home.

3. Someone will use/smoke drugs and thinks you are being an old humbug when you object or, in my case, throw a complete wobbly.

4. Someone will string you along about not being able to pay rent when, in reality, they've just blown it on a holiday/ new phone/ hot date.

5. No one will think the damp patch on the ceiling, which grows bigger every day, is worth mentioning.

6. Hall and landing light bulbs and shades will mysteriously disappear as no one can be bothered to find the spares in the kitchen drawer.

7. It's no-one's fault that the kitchen bin hasn't been emptied for a week.

8. Make good friends with a mattress supplier - you will need to replace them after most lets. DO NOT TRY TO GUESS WHAT THE STAINS ARE!

9. You will be called late on a Saturday night from a tenant trying to speed dial a taxi/takeaway/ girlfriend depending where you are listed in his

phone book. (I was once called at midnight by a tenant who described all the naughty things he was going to do to me once he got home from the pub. He was mortified the next day as he thought he'd called his girlfriend as we share the same initial. Until that point, I was rather flattered).

10. You will spend your spare hours redirecting post and bailiffs for ex tenants.

HMOS - NOW EVERYONE'S AT IT

Not so long ago, as an HMO Landlady, I was looked upon as the poor relation in landlord terms. I would attend meetings and be one of the only HMO landlords NOT housing students and my peers would sniff disdainfully or snigger as I defended my market. How the world is a-changing... (well, my world - I think the actual world has enough on its plate).

This week I was asked to advise a landlord who was hoping to rent to students but has changed market due to an oversupply of accommodation and our town's university cheekily about to charge the same annual fees as Oxford and Cambridge - talk about delusions of adequacy. I was flattered that he'd asked me to help give him some tips and advise the layout - no one's normally interested when I wax lyrical about HMOs. He told me he was going to place the ad online to attract only working people and presumably to deter anyone not suitable from seeing the ad in print as they wrap the newspaper around their bottle of vodka. He's going to do just fine as he'd already decided on a comprehensive referencing technique and drawn up room contracts - it took me 2 years to get to that stage!

Then, I was asked by a letting agent to look at a six bedroomed house that he'd been asked to tenant. OK house, OK rooms but with a prevailing smell of damp, unfinished bathrooms, but all the fire regs were in place and the landlord wanted £400 pm PLUS bills. Now, bearing in mind my most expensive room is £100 pw including all bills for a huge room, that's steep. He also revealed that the landlord was trying to raise £2.5 million to buy more HMOs.

The next call came from someone wanting to give out my number to a family member who wants to get into HMOs for their yield. In the five years I've been operating HMOs not ONE landlord has ever thought it was a good idea to let property this way and advised me to jump ship in favour of students. (Not my market of choice due to their lack of domestic skills - even my own children manage to clear up after themselves). They didn't understand that, buying at the height of the property boom in 2007 meant I HAD to do HMOs otherwise the buildings couldn't pay.

The Effect

So, for five years I've been paddling away, becoming accustomed to the sneers, riding the storms with the help of my landlord association saying "Well, what did you expect?" and having many moments of wanting to winch myself to safety to hold down a normal job. Judging by the number of ads in the paper this week, lots of landlords are riding the Room Letting wave - but will they stick with it?

I put an ad in the paper this week and only received two calls: one from a bloke who, asked where he's living now, said "On the street" and it took every ounce of will to tell him I couldn't help and hang up. For the next half hour I was going to call him back, but my head took over to remind me how many times I've been proverbially shafted by the homeless over the years.

The next respondee was Ashley: he told me his ex-girlfriend was having an affair and managed to get him sectioned based on false evidence of depression and self harm with a supporting testimonial from his mum. He has now been released and is being housed in a B&B at a cost to Housing Benefit of £140 pw plus a top up of £40 pw and an £18 pw service charge. Perhaps I could throw in a bowl of cornflakes and a cuppa every morning and charge £198 pw! To summarise: plausible story, the first I've ever heard involving sectioning and, as I've said before I'm a sucker for a sob story. Unfortunately, he failed my referencing test - he couldn't look me in the eye without jumping from one leg to another.

Will there ever be an end to the HMO bubble? Unlikely. Pressure on good accommodation is increasing, people are having to adjust their expectations of what they can afford and, let's face it, renting rooms is one of the oldest markets in the world! My last ad for a room to rent elicited over 20 enquiries from potentially good tenants - this is one industry you can guarantee strong market demand for the foreseeable future.

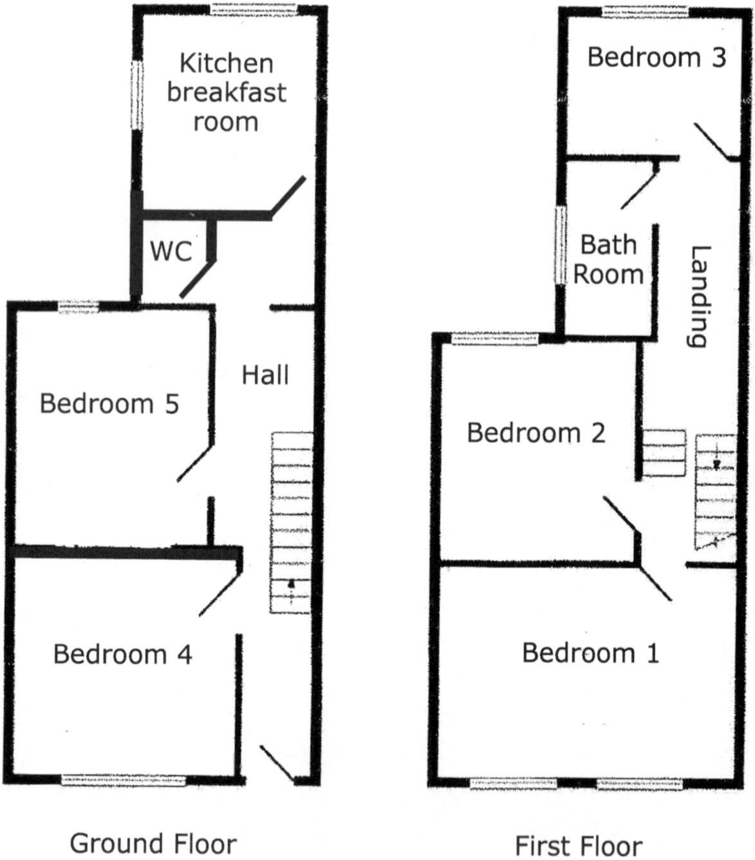

Typical floor plan of a Victorian terraced house arranged as an HMO

An invitation

We are looking for authors who would like to write a book for this series, called SUSSED.

We have created a book structure to help you get going. See: **www.colophonprint.com**

You may have other interests that you could share with the world. You may have friends that have something to say.

Please get in touch and let's talk about it.

Remember too many more books are likely to be sold in the eBook format than in traditional printed form.

SUSSED

100 Pages of Personal Experience

The SUSSED series

"SUSSED" is the generic name for a series of unique, easy-to-understand, quick-read knowledge guides across a wide variety of useful subjects published by Colophon in print and ebook format. The books are deliberately terse and snappy, presented mostly in point form so that even for absolute beginners, information is understood and picked up quickly. To ensure content is brief and relevant, length is constrained to a trademark 100 pages.

The Subjects
Sussed books are for everyday people facing everyday issues. Their subjects are practical, emotional, or social, drawn from direct experience. They have a familiarity that everyone shares, a know-how that stimulates immediate understanding.

Some are commonplace but relevant:
Boyfriends, Girlfriends, Apprenticeships, Online Privacy, Dating mates, Slimming, Working at Home, Parents, Running, Teenagers, Affairs.

Others are more specialised, often at a premium price:
Home Safety, Renting HMOs, Interviews, Therapy, Relationships, Moving House, Redundancy, Drug Addiction, Emigrating, Islam, Integration.

13735453R10058

Printed in Great Britain
by Amazon.co.uk, Ltd.,
Marston Gate.